PORTRAITS OF THE STATES

MICHIGAN

by Muriel L. Dubois
and Jonatha A. Brown

GARETH**STEVENS**
PUBLISHING
A Member of the WRC Media Family of Companies

Please visit our web site at: www.garethstevens.com
For a free color catalog describing Gareth Stevens Publishing's
list of high-quality books and multimedia programs, call
1-800-542-2595 (USA) or 1-800-387-3178 (Canada).
Gareth Stevens Publishing's fax: (414) 332-3567.

Library of Congress Cataloging-in-Publication Data

Dubois, Muriel L.
    Michigan / Muriel L. Dubois and Jonatha A. Brown.
      p. cm. — (Portraits of the states)
    Includes bibliographical references and index.
    ISBN 0-8368-4627-3 (lib. bdg.)
    ISBN 0-8368-4646-X (softcover)
    1. Michigan—Juvenile literature. I. Brown, Jonatha A.
  II. Title. III. Series.
  F566.3.D83   2005
  977.4—dc22   2005048967

This edition first published in 2006 by
Gareth Stevens Publishing
A Member of the WRC Media Family of Companies
330 West Olive Street, Suite 100
Milwaukee, WI 53212 USA

This edition copyright © 2006 by Gareth Stevens, Inc.

Editorial direction: Mark J. Sachner
Project manager: Jonatha A. Brown
Editor: Betsy Rasmussen
Art direction and design: Tammy West
Picture research: Diane Laska-Swanke
Indexer: Walter Kronenberg
Production: Jessica Morris and Robert Kraus

Picture credits: Cover, pp. 22, 24, 25, 26 © Gibson Stock Photography;
pp. 4, 18, 28 © James P. Rowan; pp. 5, 10, 11 © Corel; pp. 6, 8 © Art Today;
p. 9 © North Wind Picture Archives; p. 15 © PhotoDisc; p. 16 © Stephen
Dunn/Getty Images; p. 29 © Steve Kagan/Time & Life Pictures/Getty Images

Printed in the United States of America

1 2 3 4 5 6 7 8 9 09 08 07 06 05

CONTENTS

Words that are defined in the Glossary appear
in **bold** the first time they are used in the text.

On the Cover: Sleeping Bear Dunes National Lakeshore is one of
Michigan's peaceful places.

Introduction

Michigan is like two states in one! It includes two large, separate bodies of land. They are the Upper **Peninsula** and the Lower Peninsula. These two parts of the state are separated by the waters of Lake Michigan and Lake Huron.

Life in both parts of Michigan is fun all year long. People snowmobile and ski in the winter. They swim, fish, and boat in the summer. Families pick apples in the fall and go to festivals in every season. So, come to Michigan! Join the fun!

Pictured Rocks National Lakeshore is a wild area. Its high cliffs plunge down to Lake Superior.

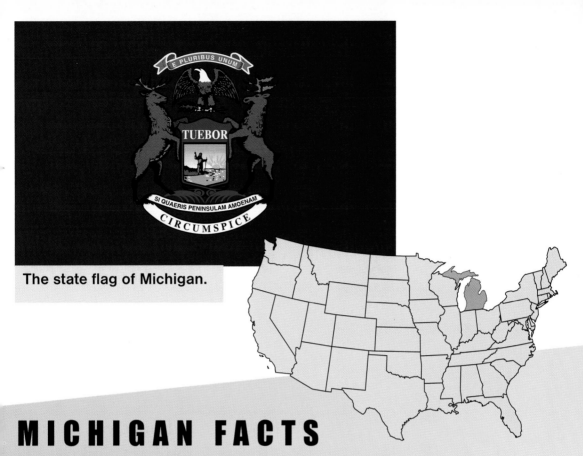

The state flag of Michigan.

MICHIGAN FACTS

- Became the 26th state: January 26, 1837
- Population (2004): 10,112,620
- Capital: Lansing
- Biggest Cities: Detroit, Grand Rapids, Warren, Flint
- Size: 56,804 square miles (147,122 square kilometers)
- Nickname: The Wolverine State
- State Tree: White pine
- State Flower: Apple blossom
- State Bird: Robin
- State Reptile: Painted turtle
- State Game Mammal: White-tailed deer

History

Native Americans came to Michigan about eleven thousand years ago. They moved from place to place to find food. They hunted with **flint** arrowheads. They fished and picked berries and nuts. Later, they learned to plant beans, corn, and squash. They gathered wild rice, too.

French Explorers

The French reached Michigan in about 1622. Étienne Brûlé was the first. He and his crew sailed west through the Great Lakes. They reached the tip of the Upper Peninsula. Other explorers followed.

Father Jacques Marquette and Louis Jolliet met many Natives as they explored the Michigan area.

Jacques Marquette, a Catholic priest, and Louis Jolliet explored Michigan. Marquette built a **mission** at Sault Ste. Marie (pronounced "soo-saint-ma-rie") in 1668. It was the first European settlement in Michigan. It lasted thirty years.

Other Catholic priests came to Michigan, too. They taught their faith to the Native people there.

French traders also arrived. They gave the Natives guns, cloth, and other goods in return for furs. Beaver fur was prized in Europe, and Michigan had plenty of beavers. The French officially claimed the area in 1671.

The British Arrive

The British explored North America, too. They founded colonies along the Atlantic Coast. Sometimes, the British and the French claimed the same land. This was the case with Michigan.

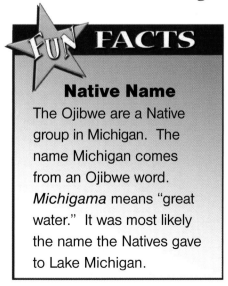

FUN FACTS

Native Name

The Ojibwe are a Native group in Michigan. The name Michigan comes from an Ojibwe word. *Michigama* means "great water." It was most likely the name the Natives gave to Lake Michigan.

Famous People of Michigan

Chief Pontiac

Born: About 1720 near the Maumee River, Ohio

Died: April 20, 1769, Cahokia, Illinois

Pontiac was a great Ottawa chief. He did not want the British to take over Native lands. In 1762, he made a war plan with other Native Americans. In the spring of 1763, they attacked twelve forts and tried to drive the British out. Pontiac's plan nearly worked. He and his men captured and destroyed eight forts. However, they failed to capture the fort at Detroit. The British held them off for more than six months. Finally, the Natives gave up. Pontiac signed a peace treaty with Great Britain a few years later.

Both countries wanted to control this region.

The two countries went to war in 1754. It was called the French and Indian War. They fought for nine years. Finally, Great Britain won. Britain now ruled thirteen colonies on the East Coast. It also held the Great Lakes area, including the area that is now Michigan.

Joining a New Country

The Atlantic colonies grew tired of British rule. They began fighting to be free in 1775. The Revolutionary War lasted eight years. The colonies finally won the war and formed the United States. This new country took control of present-day Michigan. In 1787, the Northwest Territory was created. Michigan was part of it.

In the 1800s, many people moved to Michigan to work in the iron mines.

More and more settlers moved to Michigan. Many of these people were farmers. Others worked in lumber. They harvested big trees from the forests there. Later, copper and iron ore were discovered in the northern part of Michigan. Miners began moving to Michigan, too.

Michigan became the twenty-sixth U.S. state in 1837. Detroit was its first capital. Ten years later, the capital was moved to Lansing.

Good and Bad Times

By the mid-1800s, a big disagreement had developed in the United States. People in Michigan and other northern states were against slavery. They wanted to ban slavery all over the nation. Many people in the South

The United States and Britain fought again in the War of 1812. The British held Detroit and the Great Lakes for more than one year. Finally, the U.S. Navy won the Battle of Lake Erie. This win brought the area back under U.S. control.

FUN FACTS

Travel Grows Easier

In the early 1800s, the first useful steamships were built. They traveled back and forth between Detroit, Michigan and Buffalo, New York. In 1825, the Erie **Canal** opened in New York State. Now there was a water route all the way from New York City to Detroit. These changes made it easier for people to travel to Michigan.

Detroit became a busy city in the 1800s. Its location on Lake Erie made it an important port.

disagreed. They used slaves to work on their farms. The South started their own nation called the Confederate States of America. The North did not want to split. The two sides started the Civil War in 1861. They fought for four years. Michigan sided with the North. Finally, the North won. Slavery was banned, and the South rejoined the United States.

Life in Michigan changed after the war. More and more machines did work that had once been done by hand. **Factories** sprang up around the state. People came to the cities to work in the factories. They made chemicals, cement, and other goods. In the 1900s,

FACTS

"Horseless Carriages"

In 1896, three men in Michigan started making "horseless carriages," or cars. Charles King was one of them. Henry Ford was another. The third was Ransom Olds. These men put gasoline engines on wagons. Now the wagons could run under their own power. They did not need to be pulled by horses. Cars soon became popular. By the late 1920s, auto factories in Michigan were building three-fourths of the cars in the country.

factories in Michigan began to make cars. Cars became the state's main product.

The United States entered World War I in 1917. Michigan factories helped in the war effort. They made airplane engines, trucks, and supplies.

Workers and Their Problems

In the 1930s, the whole country suffered through the **Great Depression**. Millions of people were out of work. Most could not afford to buy cars. About half of the auto workers in Michigan lost their jobs. Those who kept

Henry Ford's Model T was the most popular car in the world in the early 1900s.

their jobs usually worked long hours for low pay. Many worked in unsafe places. Workers who complained could be fired.

In the mid-1930s, auto workers formed **labor unions**. Unions stood up for workers. They made bosses and owners treat workers more fairly. Unions soon grew powerful in Michigan and other states. They helped workers get higher pay and shorter working hours.

More Ups and Downs

The United States entered World War II in 1941. Factories made equipment and supplies. The war brought jobs to the state and helped Michigan recover from the Depression.

After the war, people bought more cars. This buying was good for Michigan. It created more jobs in auto factories. Later, cars from other countries became popular, and some factories in the state had to close.

Today, the state welcomes many new businesses. In fact, it recently led the nation in the number of new buildings for businesses.

IN MICHIGAN'S HISTORY

Flint Workers Take a Stand

Factory owners did not like unions. They did not want unions telling them what to do. Some bosses fired workers just for talking about joining a union. In 1936, workers in Flint held a **strike**. They refused to work until they were allowed to join a union. The strike lasted for forty-four days. Finally, the factory owners gave in. They let the workers join a union. Now, the workers could band together and work for change.

About 1622	Étienne Brûlé sails to the Sault Ste. Marie area.
1668	Jacques Marquette builds a settlement at Sault Ste. Marie.
1701	Antoine de la Mothe Cadillac founds Detroit.
1763	Great Britain wins the French and Indian War and takes control of Michigan.
1783	Britain gives up Michigan to the United States.
1812	The British take over Detroit during the War of 1812.
1837	Michigan becomes a U.S. state.
1896	Three Michigan men build cars.
1917	U.S. involvement in World War I begins.
1936	Autoworkers strike in Flint.
1941	U.S. involvement in World War II begins.
1967	**Race riots** break out in Detroit.
1990	Several auto plants close in Michigan.
2003 and 2004	Named the number two state in the country for a positive business climate.

People

More than ten million people live in Michigan. Most of them live in the Lower Peninsula. The Upper Peninsula has far fewer people.

Almost three-fourths of the state's people live in or near cities. Detroit is the largest city. More than half of the people in the state live there. Yet Detroit is shrinking. Flint and other cities are shrinking, too. Many people are now moving to small towns. Some small towns are growing faster than cities.

Hispanics: In the 2000 U.S. Census, 3.3 percent of the people living in Michigan called themselves Latino or Hispanic. Most of them or their relatives came from places where Spanish is spoken. They may come from different racial backgrounds.

The People of Michigan

Total Population 10,112,620

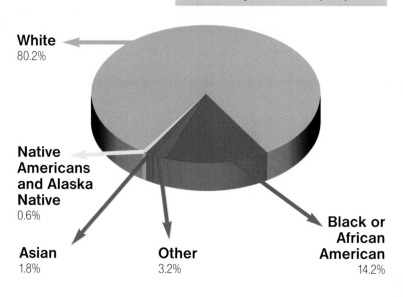

White
80.2%

Native Americans and Alaska Native
0.6%

Asian
1.8%

Other
3.2%

Black or African American
14.2%

Percentages are based on 2000 Census.

Home to Many Cultures

Many Europeans came to the state in the mid-1800s. Newcomers often settled near other people from their home countries. Many Germans and Poles moved to Detroit. The Dutch settled in the western part of the state. People from Finland lived in the Upper Peninsula.

People are still coming to Michigan from far away. In the last few years, many have come from India and the Middle East. Others have come from Latin America.

Large numbers of African Americans moved to Michigan in the 1900s. Today, more than half of the black people in the state live in Detroit. There have sometimes been problems between different racial groups there. In 1943 and 1967, race riots broke out in

Detroit is home to the largest number of African Americans in any city in Michigan.

Detroit. Dozens of people died. Since then, Michigan has worked to solve problems among people of different races.

Today, very few Natives live in Michigan. In the 1800s, settlers pushed most of them out of the state. Many of those who remain now live on **reservations**.

Most Native Americans living there today are Ojibwe.

Religion and Education

Most people in the state are Christians. The largest Protestant group is Baptist. Presbyterians, Episcopalians, and other Protestant faiths can also be found there. About one-fourth of the people in the state are Catholic. Jews, Muslims, Hindus, and Buddhists live in the state, too.

College football has many fans in Michigan. Here, the University of Michigan Wolverines play the Texas Longhorns.

Famous People of Michigan

John Harvey Kellogg

Born: February 26, 1852, Tyrone, Michigan

Died: December 14, 1943, Battle Creek, Michigan

William Keith Kellogg

Born: April 7, 1860, Battle Creek, Michigan

Died: October 6, 1951, Battle Creek, Michigan

The Kellogg brothers were not the first people to make cereal flakes, but they were the first to sell them as a breakfast food. John was a doctor who ran a health center. He wanted his patients to have a healthy diet. For breakfast, he began serving them flaked corn or wheat. His brother, William, liked the idea. He founded a company to sell cereals as breakfast food. In 1894, his company started selling wheat flakes. Today, the Kellogg Company makes all kinds of breakfast cereals.

Michigan was the first U.S. state to set up public high schools. It was also one of the first to have public libraries. Today, the state has many fine colleges. In fact, Michigan has more than one hundred colleges and universities. The University of Michigan is the oldest. Its **campus** at Ann Arbor is one of the top universities in the nation. Michigan State University in East Lansing is also well known. It was the first college in the country to teach farming. Northern Michigan University in Marquette is home to the U.S. Olympic Education Center. Athletes skate, run track, and learn other sports.

17

The Land

A peninsula is a piece of land that has water on three sides. Michigan is two big peninsulas. One forms the northern part of the state. The other forms the southern part. In both, the climate is cool and wet. Summers are mild. Winter temperatures often dip well below freezing.

The Upper Peninsula

The Upper Peninsula is in the north. It is often called the U.P. The U.P. borders on three of the five Great Lakes. They are Lake Superior, Lake Michigan, and Lake Huron.

The Sleeping Bear Dunes overlook Lake Michigan.

MICHIGAN

Keweenaw
NHP

Keweenaw
Peninsula

LAKE SUPERIOR

CANADA

Keweenaw Bay

L. Gogebic

Pictured
Rocks NL

Grand
Island

Mt. Arvon

*SUPERIOR
UPLAND*

Marquette •

National Ski
Hall of Fame

Sault Ste. Marie •

*CENTRAL
LOWLAND*

Father Marquette
National Memorial

Fayette
Historical
Townsite

Menominee R.

Straits Of Mackinac

Beaver
Island

Grand Traverse Bay

*Green
Bay*

Sleeping Bear
Dunes NL

L. Charlevoix

Thunder
Bay

LAKE HURON

N
W   **E**
S

Au Sable R.

Manistee R.

Higgins L.

Muskegon R.

Hardy
Dam
Pond

Saginaw
Bay

Bay City •

Cass R.

WISCONSIN

CENTRAL LOWLAND

Frankenmuth •

Grand R.
Grand Rapids

• Flint

LAKE MICHIGAN

• Holland

Lansing

Warren •

Pontiac •   • Troy

E. Lansing

Battle Creek •

Detroit •

*L.
St. Clair*

• Kalamazoo

Ann Arbor •

Dearborn •

ILLINOIS

St. Joseph R.

INDIANA   **OHIO**

LAKE ERIE

SCALE/KEY

0	100 Miles
0	100 Kilometers

⊛ State Capital

▲ Highest Point

▨ Mountains

FUN FACTS

The Wolverine State

Michigan is known as "The Wolverine State." Wolverines are large, mean animals in the **weasel** family. Oddly, wolverines have never lived in this state! Some people say that people in Ohio used the nickname first. They may have said that Michigan folks were as mean and nasty as wolverines! Another tale says that Native people called settlers "wolverines." The settlers gobbled up land just like wolverines gobble their food. No one knows if either story is true.

Major Rivers

Grand River
260 miles (418 km) long

Muskegon River
200 miles (322 km) long

St. Joseph River
210 miles (338 km) long

The western part of the U.P. is a rugged area. Mount Arvon is in this region. At 1,979 feet (603 meters), it is the highest point in Michigan. Much of the land in this part of the state is covered with forests and swamps. Copper and iron were once mined there.

Further east, the land is mostly level, and the soil is sandy. Some of this land is used for farming.

Bears, moose, and gray wolves can be found in the U.P. Beavers live here, too, along with many other small animals. Wild turkeys, quail, and grouse are some of the common birds.

The Lower Peninsula

The Lower Peninsula is often called the "Mitten." The

name is fitting because this part of the state is shaped like a big mitten. It touches Lakes Michigan, Huron, and Erie. A chunk of land that sticks out into Lake Huron is called the "thumb."

Land in the Mitten is flat in some places and has rolling hills in others. Toward the north, the soil is sandy. Beautiful sand beaches line parts of the Lake Michigan shore. Further south, the soil is clay. The state's major cities are in this part of the state.

The Mitten was once covered with forests. Most of the trees were cut down long ago. Then, people began replanting trees. Now, more than half of the land has pine and fir trees.

Deer, foxes, beavers, and many smaller animals live in the Mitten. Every fall and spring, thousands of ducks and other waterbirds stop along the shores of Lake Erie.

Lakes and Rivers

Michigan has the longest freshwater shoreline in the world. It is also the only U.S. state that touches four of the five Great Lakes. They are the largest lakes in North America. The state has more than eleven thousand inland lakes, too. Torch Lake is one, and many people say it is one of the loveliest lakes in the world.

Michigan has many rivers. Most run through the southern part of the Mitten. Many of the rivers are narrow and not very deep. Some have rapids and waterfalls. Ships cannot use these rivers, but **tourists** enjoy them. They catch trout, walleye, salmon, and other fish.

Economy

Many people in Michigan work in factories. Cars are the main items produced there. Car factories employ one-third of all factory workers in the state. When many people are buying cars from Michigan, jobs are plentiful. When car sales are down, many people are out of work. In the late 1970s and early 1980s, car sales were down. More people were out of work in Michigan than in any other U.S. state.

Factories in Michigan produce other goods, too. Some build machinery and furniture. Others make cereal and baby food.

Michigan factories have been building cars for a long time. These old cars and planes are in a museum in Dearborn.

Farming, Mining, and Tourism

The top field crop is corn. The state also produces fruits and vegetables. Michigan produces more cucumbers and sour cherries than any other state. It is also a leader in blueberry, sweet cherry, and dry bean production. Apples and Christmas trees are important crops, too. Grains are grown in the south. Potatoes grow in the north.

Tourists bring a great deal of money into the state. They go to national forests, rivers, and lakes. They visit parks and museums. Tourists also stay in motels and eat at restaurants. All of these places need workers.

Copper and iron mining were once important in Michigan, but few mines are open today. Michigan still mines some iron ore.

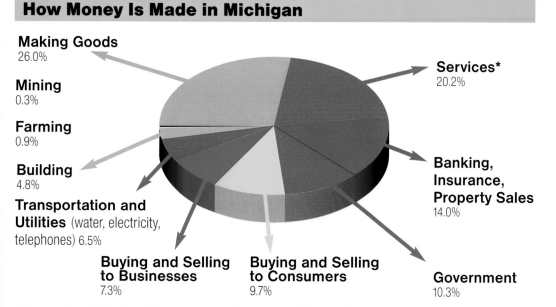

How Money Is Made in Michigan

Making Goods
26.0%

Mining
0.3%

Farming
0.9%

Building
4.8%

Transportation and Utilities (water, electricity, telephones) 6.5%

Buying and Selling to Businesses
7.3%

Buying and Selling to Consumers
9.7%

Services*
20.2%

Banking, Insurance, Property Sales
14.0%

Government
10.3%

* Services include jobs in hotels, restaurants, auto repair, medicine, teaching, and entertainment.

Government

L ansing is the capital of Michigan. The state's leaders work there. The state government has three parts, or branches. They are the executive, legislative, and judicial branches.

Executive Branch

The executive branch sees that state laws are carried out. The governor is the head of this branch. The lieutenant governor helps. A team of people called the **cabinet** also help the governor.

Michigan's State Capitol Building is in Lansing. This building was finished in 1879.

The inside of the State Capitol Building is very grand. The House of Representatives meets in this room to make state laws.

Judicial Branch

Judges and courts make up the judicial branch. When someone is accused of committing a crime, they may decide whether the person is guilty.

County Governments

Michigan is divided into eighty-three counties. Each county is run by a group of people known as a board of **commissioners**.

Legislative Branch

The state legislature is called the General Assembly. It has two parts. They are the Senate and the House of Representatives. These two parts work together to make state laws.

MICHIGAN'S STATE GOVERNMENT

Executive		Legislative		Judicial	
Office	**Length of Term**	**Body**	**Length of Term**	**Court**	**Length of Term**
Governor	4 years	Senate (38 members)	4 years	Supreme Court (7 justices)	8 years
Lieutenant Governor	4 years	House of Representatives (110 members)	2 years	Appeals court (28 judges)	6 years

Things to See and Do

The Grand Haven lighthouse is on Lake Michigan. It is often called "Big Red."

People who enjoy the outdoors love Michigan! It has more publicly owned forests than any other state in the Midwest and the East. It has more than ninety state parks, too. Visitors to the state can fish, hike, camp, and swim. They can also hunt, ice skate, and cross-country ski.

The Frederik Meijer Gardens and **Sculpture** Park is in Grand Rapids. Colorful plants bloom indoors and out. Sculptures dot the grounds. One is of a bronze horse. At 24 feet (7 m) high, it is the largest bronze horse in the world. Its creator got the idea for the horse from Leonardo da Vinci, an artist who lived long ago.

Madonna

Born: August 16, 1958, Bay City, Michigan

Madonna Louise Ciccone is known to most people as Madonna. She is one of the most popular pop/rock stars in the world. Her first hit song, "Holiday," came out in 1983. Later, she was one of the first singers to make music videos. She has acted in movies, too. In 1996, she starred in *Evita*. This movie won many awards. In the past few years, she has written a number of children's books.

Michigan has plenty of indoor fun, especially in Detroit. The city is known for its theaters and museums. People go to shows, listen to live music, and enjoy art. Kalamazoo and Grand Rapids also have good art museums. Lansing has a wonderful history museum.

Sports

In college football and basketball, Michigan State and the University of Michigan are nationally known rivals. Michigan Tech is a hockey powerhouse.

The state also has many big-league sports teams. Detroit is home to all of these teams. The Tigers play baseball, and the Lions play football. Each year, the Lions play a home game on Thanksgiving Day.

Hockey fans in the state are proud of the Red Wings. They have won the Stanley Cup several times, most recently in 2002. Basketball fans have a lot to cheer about, too. The men's team, the Detroit Pistons, have won the National Basketball Association

Famous People of Michigan

Joe Louis

Born: May 13, 1914, Lafayette, Alabama

Died: April 12, 1981, Las Vegas, Nevada

Joe Louis was an African American boxer. He started his career in Detroit. He was called "The Brown Bomber." Louis was quick but calm. In 1936, he lost a fight to Max Schmeling, a German. The leader of Germany, Adolf Hitler, thought Germans were better than anyone else on Earth. He thought Schmeling's win proved it. Louis fought Schmeling again in 1938. This time, Louis knocked him out in the first round! He was the Heavyweight Boxing Champion for twelve years. He fought seventy-two times as a professional and lost only three matches.

Dearborn is the home of the Henry Ford Museum.

Women's National Basketball Association (WNBA) champs in 2003.

Festivals and Fairs

People enjoy festivals all over Michigan. Ann Arbor is known for its huge arts fair. The city of Holland

(NBA) title in recent years. The women's team, the Detroit Shock, were

Motown singers crowd around a piano and belt out a tune in the 1960s.

FACTS

The Motown Sound

Detroit was home to a new singing style in the 1960s. This style was called "Motown." The name came from Detroit's nickname, which was Motor City. Stevie Wonder, the Jackson Five, the Supremes, the Temptations, and the Four Tops were famous Motown singing acts.

holds the Tulip Festival in May. Visitors see beautiful flowers in bloom. They learn about Dutch culture. Frankenmuth hosts a Bavarian Festival in June. People eat German foods and listen to live music. They watch parades and go on rides.

★ ★

cabinet — a team of people who help a leader make decisions

campus — the grounds on which a university is built

canal — an artificial river

commissioners — members of government groups or departments

factories — buildings where goods and products are made

flint — a hard gray stone

Great Depression — a time in the 1930s when many people and businesses lost money

labor unions — groups that try to make pay and working conditions better for workers in a factory or other business

mission — a church

peninsula — land that is nearly surrounded by water

race riots — wild, violent acts by crowds of people usually caused by anger about a difference in treatment of different groups of people

reservations — lands set apart by the government for a certain purpose

sculpture — a statue carved from stone, metal, wood, marble, or clay

strike — to refuse to work because of a disagreement between employers and employees

tourists — people who travel for pleasure

weasel — a small mammal with a long slender body

Books

Go Big Blue: The Michigan Wolverines Story. Neal Bernards (The Creative Company)

Lake Michigan. Anne Ylvisaker (Capstone Press)

Legend of the Petoskey Stone. Kathy-Jo Wargin (Sleeping Bear Press)

M is for Mitten: A Michigan Alphabet Book. Annie Appleford and Kathy-Jo Wargin (Thomson Gale)

Michigan. Johannah Haney (Marshall Cavendish, Inc.)

Michigan Native People. Marcia Shonberg (Heinemann Library)

Web Sites

MI Kids! Michigan government Web site for kids
www.michigan.gov/mikids

Michigan Department of Agriculture
www.mda.state.mi.us/kids/index.html

Michigan Department of Natural Resources
www.outdoorexplorersclub.com/flash/OECKids/
KidsMain.html

INDEX